I0801080

Catch a Fish

LEVEL 4

/er/ar/

DECODABLES BY jump!

Teaching Tips

Blue Level 4

This book focuses on the phonemes **/er/ar/**.

Before Reading

- Discuss the title. Ask readers what they think the book will be about. Have them briefly explain why.
- Ask readers to sort the words on page 3. Read the sounds and words together.

Read the Book

- Encourage readers to break down unfamiliar words into units of sound. Then, ask them to string the sounds together to create the words.
- Urge readers to point out when the focused phonics phonemes appear in the text.

After Reading

- Encourage children to reread the book independently or with a friend.
- Ask readers to name other words with /er/ or /ar/ phonemes. On a separate sheet of paper, have them write the words out.

North American adaptations © 2024 Jump!
5357 Penn Avenue South
Minneapolis, MN 55419
www.jumplibrary.com

Library of Congress Cataloging-in-Publication Data is available at www.loc.gov or upon request from the publisher.

ISBN: 979-8-88996-819-1 (hardcover)
ISBN: 979-8-88996-820-7 (paperback)
ISBN: 979-8-88996-821-4 (ebook)

Photo Credits

Images are courtesy of Shutterstock.com. With thanks to Getty Images, Thinkstock Photo and iStockphoto. Cover – Matt Jeppson. 4–5 – Monkey Business Images, Roman Chazov. 6–7 – Ashley Swanson, Haiduchyk Aliaksei. 8–9 – Giovenda, Ixepop. 10–11 – AT Production, Roman Choknadii. 12–13 – Tatiana Bobkova, Videohotdogs. 14–15 – Dean Drobot, RossHelen. 16 – Shutterstock.

Can you sort all the words on this page into two groups?

Farm

Fern

Words with
er

Perch

Card

Jar

Words with
ar

Harp

Herd

Do you ever go out to fish?

You can get a spot next to a river to wait for the fish.

If you have a chair, sit on that. If not, sit on the dock.

Do you have a rod? A rod can catch fish from afar.

Get some bait and get it on the hook.

The hook and bait go in the river.
Now you wait for a fish.

Wait for a fish to tug. If the rod bends, you might have one.

Reel the fish in. Then see what kind it is. Is it big or little?

If you catch a little fish, you can toss it back.

If you catch a big fish, you can have it for lunch!

Keep the fish cool when you get it. This will keep it fresh.

You can char the fish on a grill when you get back. Yum!

Sound out each word. Does it have an /er/ or /ar/ sound?

barn

tiger

scarf

butter